GW00399948

The Land Between

Also by Wendy Mulford:

POETRY

Bravo to Girls and Heroes (1977)

No Fee: A Line or Two for Free (with Denise Riley) (1978)

The Light Sleepers (1980)

Reactions to Sunsets (1980)

River Whose Eyes (1982)

Some Poems (with Denise Riley) (1982)

The ABC of Writing and other poems (1985)

Late Spring Next Year: Poems 1979-84 (1987)

Lusus Naturae (1990)

Nevrazumitelny (1991)

The Bay of Naples (1992)

The East Anglia Sequence (1998)

and suddenly, supposing: Selected Poems (2002)

Whistling Through the Nightwood (with Anne Beresford, Herbert Lomas
        & Pauline Stainer (2008)

PROSE

This Narrow Place: Sylvia Townsend Warner and Valentine Ackland (1988)

Virtuous Magic: women saints and their meanings (with Sara Maitland) (1998)

TRANSLATION

The Brontes Hats by Sarah Kirsch (with Anthony Vivis) (1992)

T by Sarah Kirsch (with Antony Vivis) (1995)

EDITOR

The Virago Book of Love Poetry (1990, 1998)

The Land
Between

Wendy Mulford

REALITY STREET
2009

Published by
REALITY STREET
63 All Saints Street, Hastings, East Sussex TN34 3BN
www.realitystreet.co.uk

Copyright © Wendy Mulford, 2009

Cover image: *The Pine, Hawk and Glossy Ganoderma*, by Giuseppe Castiglione (Chinese name Lang Shining) (1688-1766), hanging scroll, colour on silk,. The Palace Museum, Beijing

Book design and typesetting: Ken Edwards

Printed and bound in Great Britain by CPI Antony Rowe, Chippenham and Eastbourne

A catalogue record for this book is available from the British Library

ISBN: 978-1-874400-44-8

ACKNOWLEDGEMENTS
Some of these poems have appeared in *La Traductière, Artworld, Poetry Wales, Scintilla* and *Moment of Earth: Poems & Essays in Honour of Jeremy Hooker.*

For Jean Crozier and for Denise Riley

In memory of Noel Haden Bevan, priest,
31 October 1934–8 April 2008

Part I

I CHINA AM 7

i   longevity speaks
ii   the heart / the underworld
iii   Commence inkstone
iv   Only the hound

Part II

Poems 2008..19

Crumbling pence
One-way conversations
Broken
Winding back the newsreel

Part III

Poems 2002-08 41

from The Chinese Postcard Sequence
poems for ARTWORLD: After Peter Doig
Poem-sculpture sur prose
The Withyman
In the East
Stockings and Whisky
At Thorpeness
The Question
Yr Heniath
Parallel existences

Part I

我中國是

I CHINA AM

i

longevity speaks

        fragile you

             entered

seal script unfolded

       an underslip

a waterway

     leading

           nowhere

baffles

      ripe

           pomegranate

jade

   (d)

       linghzi

    solitary   *salute*

      ***

I China am

    silent presence   *am*

brushing the silk

    inside   *your elbow*

how

    an ear-lobe hangs

Bodhsivatta

    a cartuche

         bronze bodies

to exchange in the

    Heavenly Kingdom

female   *I unfurl the*

    Underworld

each mark the

    hawk hangs

the

    body-map

    turquoise

slays my universe

    led

    blessings the

dragon bestowed for

    tranquillity restored

shorn from the

    lacquered halls

flames stepping & the

    Mother of God

    prays

***

floating silk

    pellucid screens

        yield to

military guise

    wounds

        the scholar

poet

    incomplete knowledge

        broken

science

    wisdom bodes slant

        shapes the

shaman's skull

    or a wandering monk

who is revealed

    you need to know for

blue vessels likely

    limn the horizon

what matters yearning

    for trackless

        journeys

show

    the stupid inkstone

        stability's a

monochrome

    events   opening

upon a

    habit of

        not hearing

as the words   run out

ii

the heart

        the underworld

                each marks

the place is it

        me speaking   can you

colour that dragon who's

                strayed into

the universe scoops

          blessings tucked

into the nine

       fuck

           tranquillity's

fetched up

       Whooo

             flares happiness

which day   which

        night   which moon

the Jesuits floss

        smile a

                possible

self designs the

        floating silk

                reliant

upon

        the stars and

            heavenly courses

if the scholar

        poet   strays

              come back

the Altars of Earth

        yellow, red, blue

Commence

        INKSTONE *apply*

                the

  lifetime

      habit to

               open up

  the scroll

      of the Dead

              review

Perfect Brightness

              revivify

  ceramic

      porcelain

             stone

                shall signify

the New Year's

      observance

              a

one-handed

      furrow

              then

***

the instructions

        elsewhere

                      rises

very ancient

        ancestors   *bamboo*

                    flute

        cranes

are offering

        the surround is

ruby

        peach

                  the robe officially

in the place of

          the fire-eater

Auspicions

        remember in the

                  Palace

perfection attends each

              brush-stroke

else the

        orders awry

              blessed

raider and the

          fire-clawed

reliquary

       relinquish

             your hold

no more

       world   ruler

iii

Only the hound
          brushing past
                    keenly
scents
          the last
                restless
                    that's
deposited
          innumerable
                    hangings
seals
          calligraphics   the
                    virtuous
ambition's trove
                store's recollection
believe otherwise
                the fragile
fisherman's raft what's
                organic
                    decays

are you tempted
        to be assiduous
turn aside
      from borrowed music
chimes
      bells
          dogmatic treatise
jewelled movement
         the erstwhile
monuments
      of the literati
    so many shades of
       silence

The characters in the title are intentionally ungrammatical Chinese.

Composed for performance (voice and music-drone) at the Arnolfini Gallery, Bristol, December 2006, for the inauguration of the Black Mountain College anniversary exhibition.

Part II

Poems 2008

Crumbling pence, ebbing tide

pages hours wallpaper wakefulness
filling the width of the page avoiding the pavement cracks
tidied away between high-stacked houses
people on top people behind people around
asking asking asking talking talking talking
incessant sounds incessant r e-
quests demands repartee narratives songs noise
around and around and around. Surround. Pages and hours and mornings and
fearfulness soreness and wounds foreground to background and
fore again stabbing each
bored thud of the sea start at the top
angled nakedness

unplugged undrugged buried
whose food whose flesh music and image of
friendliness thorough
pages and hours and daemons and mindfulness
stolidly snap into darkness pages and hours dry-eyed remain.
Skin-fingering toe-crawling bedside blankness
underneath the unwanted world admonishing
someone wet your cheek someone offered refreshment
the handhold's gone there's no cocktail to buy
one last light.
snap. trap. darkness. Your dying was robbed you.
We remember

when being was easy, was that you dialoguing
why can't I tell which scream was your voice, there's no chords,
no-one was there, the carpet's unseated, I've guessed what I missed
was The Moment, too vast to be realised, what's ebbed is obeying
some untold law. I should have known. You suppose
a scientific or at least an economic solution.
And that's not there.
PAGES, HOURS, DEBRIS, WAKEFULNESS
that's the sentence whoever comes by.
Nearness is cancelled intimacy hideous
who believes the pines stand alone waiting sunsets
when the terror-tornado swathes through town it's
not my business I'm meeting my deadlines.
If this is called life tell me who cancelled it

Lights switch on and off car doors open to close
people come home to brick houses and draw curtains
and the small screen banishes the economy's woes.
Me I'm just measuring the last of the light.

One-way conversations

for Ken Edwards

1.
Let us imagine, for the sake of an interlocutor,
a box. A, conceptual, box. If you like, a
metaphysical box. Justified. It measures,
perhaps, six by four centimetres. A reasonable
size. It has to be filled. It probably
spawns others. Now find the words.

2.
A life without words. Sea-flakes.
skin-flakes. nail-clippings. detritus
from the hairbrush. domestic arcana.
no concern. free-sweep. rolling
the eyes. the angle's acute. Possibly.

3.
She's unavailable. It all goes in.
So familiar to place the details
in the boxes promptly provided.
The Buddhist wants us to regard terror
with an open and friendly heart
straight in the eye, no boxes.

4.
A life lived outside the box
makes me nervous & happy.
The girls are discussing their favourite
villains, passionately. He's a nasty
evil man. She speaks with authority
it's all on TV.

5.
It's wet November. They're all ready
for Christmas. The meal's been planned
and cooked several times over.
Conceptually. Conception. Ciao.
Hot air tears through my head.
I wish you'd come back. I'd
parade my makeover whilst you
pretend to notice reading the Guardian.

6.
My fingertips throb in slices.
The art of cooking is only ever
to cook what you lust for dream
over smell & taste in the wasting hours
That's oysters and soda bread guinness
& curried parsnip soup in no
particular order but not whatever
you say, Shi-rimps, Mrs Arris.

7.
Conceptually, did you count
the number of boxes – and what of the
stock – now is the moment –
turn up the stove – let the sleeping dog
disregard whose groans – disdain
the tape-measure. Close the day.

Broken

The years huddle behind me.
It is one long rhythm. Attachment and death.
Death and attachment.
Death in the middle.
Attachment, death in the wings.
Ravenless in the ravine of Kerrith.
Thankful for Oil whatever the politics.

"men go to war to prove they are as brave as women"

Make the type bigger, the blackbird calls

It is the blackest, thick ink
I found in your study. For a man who
laboured to write. Imperishable.
To register what counts. Life &
Death. Birth. Baptism. Marriage.
No subtitles. The rain falls. Steadily.
Each day. To replenish the water butts.

I visit the sea-house.
The wind rattles and groans.
My friend lifts me from the arms of
the angel. Veiled life switches on.
I descend the steep stairs. The angel plays
Das Lied von der Erde fluttering at my shoulder

I throw the dice.
Consolation or consolation.
There is only one I want.
You.
Love is a four-letter word. Now
You are a trinity

It is a wretched thing to be sybil.
There is no futurity.
You are not my child, but without
the unknown there is no shadow, no
substance. Whispers, no light,
no warmth. If it is called life it is
unworthy of the name.
In their corners arms aloft
Only love and death are equal
Close the day.

Winding back the newsreel

We have not kissed, we have not said goodbye

In the house of birth there cannot be
news of death –
at the point where the belly splits
walnut-fashion its hard
load stretching the parachute skin –
She does not want to hear of death.
Death pours from my mouth, drips
from my eyes my lips
taste of it
it hammers in my ears, the soft sound
of the last puff of breath, soft on the lips
signalling your spirit's flight, signalling
shut-down
as swift and unremarked as a power cut.
Silence. Absence. Nothing.
Old hospital clothes on the bed.
Your unruly hair all that remains of you.
You leave me nothing. You do not say goodbye.
One soft puff and you've left on your
long journey gentle as always

Part III

Poems 2002-08

from The Chinese Postcard Sequence

i
Near the Hoansu temple

the weight of their sayings in the brilliant sky

before daybreak
contemplate the foreground
retained in granite

who retreats
top left, the
undifferentiated hills

leave your pack behind
entering the town
awed by guardians

that pump's in working order
an after-image of the hills
confirms your face

beneath the Hoansu temple
a man in violet trousers & shirt
left side missing

some particles are showing
through the roar of writing

narrowed approach
through deep shadow

fine metal transects the air
between, civic or community
purposes some go(o)d

massy stone wall, a
punctuated foreground, passage to
reading what is not

what is not near
finds our recovery, between

ii
Tientsin

disinterested cloud
gestures buoyant
under the canopy

the washing hangs out to dry
behind closed doors bureaucracy
prods the bales, patiently

boats don't depart
from the marble steps
at the water's edge

another country
another attempt, the
ponies and carts, crossed seasons

from a time-ripped window
supporting the unity of tree and roof line
against the tints of evening

are we waiting again for orders
or, just such another case,
swimming freely, off-limit

2 poems for ARTWORLD

after Peter Doig, 5 Feb-27 April 2008, Tate Britain

1
Reflection – "What does your soul look like"

you have your back to me
all I see is your feet
& rumpled trouser-legs – standing heavily
on the pond. Top of the frame.
Maybe your soul is after all a tree
Your torso's a tree too
and in the pond exotic shapes float between
the barred tree-stripes or perhaps they swim
nothing's certain in your world and everything we see's
either on the edge of becoming something else
or vanishing. You see,
your world, like mine's,
an intuition game. Heaven help the sensationists
they won't have a clue what
you're up to and I'm just guessing
after all

2.

the painters are all here today
checking you out, invisible magnifying glasses &
lens attached to their foreheads they
stumble against the guardian ropes
the east european gallery guards are young and too
preoccupied with the dating game to care.
if you're lost you can
distinguish one group from the other
by their eyes though
it's no good asking the painters, s/he always has an innocent
eye and is ignorant of all arrangements.
Meanwhile the shrewd-eyed collectors are out in force –
They are to be found in huddles, far from the paintings

Poem Sculpture/'sculpture sur prose'

from La Traductiere: revue franco-anglaise de poesie et art visuel No 25, Paris 2007

i   Trajectory
radical advances
          opening
             unevenly
          seem themselves
light   darkness

ii *Alternative/original version: (unpublished)*

pockets of silence (s)hoot the
freak
Saracen North Sound Verge Pact
Portals open up visceral whimsy
Hybrid freedom for QUAS and chaos leading
to a divide eliminating distant reference
ReResistance to a triangular nature
Human destiny Verge Trickster Fallen
Angel photographic memory in the real
dog-like illusions of the painter assertively
the
    fifth
seem themselves

Poem Sculpture poems are treated prose texts according to strict rules.

The Withyman

after John Caple

A low horizon rules
beneath the moon
the moonpath leads directly

to the silent withyman
across a crippled lake, a tongue of land
lopped and pinned

dark shapes inanimate
as clockwork bird, as Trojan horse
cry out

The withyman stands between
monster withies
stapled to unforgiving vision

In the East

The women move about the white apartment floor
shunning each other's glance
silently on undiscovered feet
they weave a pattern
absorbed in miniature adjustment
to their universe each
secretes her
singular scent
intent as humming moths sipping
the moth orchid

Stockings and Whisky

for Alice Notley, and for Herbert Lomas

What is strange is I remembered your poem, Alice, as a dream
all those years ago. You know. Your
stockings poem. But no. It was
a vision, you said. Not a dream. Of Heaven. Do you remember? It begins
'Mornings I wonder if I / can fill my stockings', and ends, my all-time
favourite ending,
'My stockings were / all that was there.'
Last night I had a dream.
We were all young. Many people. Many bags. rucksacks
no space to sit.
It was a bookshop, I think. We were all waiting for something.
Someone.
A reading? A talk? who knows.
Dreams dont interest themselves in such details.
I walked through the people
fitted the key into its padlock on the narrow door
no one looked up.
Nothing remarkable in the apartment –
it was just a room , a single bed along one wall, a balcony
overlooking waste ground.

In the waste basket, at an angle, a bottle, three-quarters empty.
Laphroaig.
Your whisky was all that was there.

At Thorpeness

"My Lover, The Sea": (The Tempest. Op. 109. Sibelius.)

I am waiting. This morning
it was Cap de Nez blue. Skimmering pale
barely blue, too light for early morning eyes.
We walked north, dog and I, up the sand strip towards the sea-kale
nursery
Where the plants bloom, sporting
mementos like those who can sustain regard, knowing,
in their unruffled fruitfulness they are
worthy, undisturbed, on their shelved shingle bed.

& then
the phone rang to say you'd all be coming, now, soon, today,
imminently: don't get me wrong, of course I want you all
to be here – that's why I came after all – but now? Right now?
Oy veh!
In any relationship there are delicate moments,
early on when a thing might go forward, might stall, or
take off into a side-turning & never really dance again. That
Sea, is how I feel it is with us.
Through three days, from near-dawn until moon-up
I have studied your moods
 your light   your colour your
approach and your recoil.
I have followed beside you adapting myself
to your pace   your remoteness &
your presence   picking up slips
of knowledge of your habits
from your daily traces   learning to
recognise your voice   your movements   your smell
imprinting them on my flesh   in my
heart
hearing them in my dreams

and when, like all lovers must be,
we are parted, I will cleave to you
& nothing and no one shall separate us.
Then a new lover with blue in her eyes
will walk beside you, open her heart and her ears to you
& discover you close to her pillow
troubling her sleep. You will slap at her feet
as you do in mischievous mood, or toss and growl
as you may, and you do, & she will try, vainly as I do,
to capture you on paper, in paint or stumbling words,
& find after all that you are snagged
beneath my jumper   nearer
the heart than I had believed possible

& should I return
after absence I may find you
strangely changed
unfamiliar   stripped
of your magic
as you might in the common light be seen
as only, entirely, essentially, nothing but
the sea:
an attribute or function of the larger concept, the seaside, the
picture postcard stuff, the place where families picnic people
shout & play beachball   dogs splash ecstatic after
invisible lobbed pebbles,
a place out-of-season for the dedicated solitaries the
company of night-shore anglers to defy the cold and the winds in
windproof zip-up nylon, for small brave
night-lit boats to bob in pursuit of remnants of catches –
a sea like any other

The Question

About the shadow and the lip
            there may be
scar tissue
            never mind that
Somewhere
            the river runs down
where's home
            the trees answer

      *

Such a poise can put the
            whole life in
question
            hesitancy holds
the clue

      *

Engage such a
            question
how do you know
            the size of the ocean?
Ask again
            then plunge

      *

If the moon rises
            above this cliff
does it rise too
            in your parlour?

*

So.   There is a clearing.
                    one tall pine   bending
in the wind's commotion.
                    Soon the heart
will make its obligatory entry
                    sighing pining creating
more commotion

                    *

There are more words here than are needed
                    . . .
And still their prison hulks disgrace us

                    *

Take me down
                    the winds
don't stop their howl

                    *

It is not the place of time to tick
                    what's worth five minutes
bliss?   a song, a tale
a joke of
                    eternity

                    *

So one leg's this side
                    the estuary runs deep and cold
we may never reach the other

Yr Heniath

stone   rock   spirit
                fossil
adnabod   another
                time

the darkness reveals the light
   in my double exile
war becomes peace   children's home
                the hill farmstead
                one way story

Parallel existences

1
There is the flip switch.
Empty damp grey air.
To make the word cross out the alphabet.
The word's black. Wordless.
Heavy.
Birds singalong to rain patter patter splash splash
Trill trill.
On parallel lines.
There's leaving & not going.
There's going & not arriving.
Stationary movement.

2
Take Fanny Mendelssohn.
  Did she
Arrive where they expected her?
Perhaps we meet at the Trois Canettes,
  For example.
Will you be revenant for this tryst?
Whose names illuminate the walls.
  You can come to the café.
Some of me will be there. Voiceless. Violet life, hup
Clip-clop through the emptied streets.

3
Urbs in rure.

There was a scented soap.
I remember.
Sandalwood.
A curved bath.
The light fled over the marshes.

4
My grandmother's trinket box.

Once a
drunken poet
fell up our basement stairs
puked into the new blue
habitat bin
& fell back on your box, grandmama
obliterating the pilgrim's feet &
chipping the blue enamel edges.
The shading tree its hanging spider claws
the obsequious stranger & most
of the pink blossom remain.
I walk across the rising plain
past the blossom and the rocks
leaving them conversing.
Who'll come this way again?

5
After all
we were not there
 in the shuttered courtyard room
framed by bougainvillea

Remember
in those days you were always with me
together or apart
After all
Paris se deroule sans nous.

OTHER TITLES FROM REALITY STREET, 1993-2009

Poetry series

1993
  Kelvin Corcoran: *Lyric Lyric*, £5.99
  Susan Gevirtz: *Taken Place*, £6.50
  Maggie O'Sullivan: *In the House of the Shaman*, £6.50
  Denise Riley: *Mop Mop Georgette*, £6.50
1994
  Allen Fisher: *Dispossession and Cure*, £6.50
1995
  Fanny Howe: *O'Clock*, £6.50
  Sarah Kirsch: *T* (O/P)
  Peter Riley: *Distant Points* (O/P)
1996
  Maggie O'Sullivan (ed.): *Out of Everywhere*, £12.50
1997
  Nicole Brossard: *Typhon Dru*, £5.50
  Cris Cheek/Sianed Jones: *Songs From Navigation* (+ audio CD), £12.50
  Lisa Robertson: *Debbie: an Epic*, £7.50*
  Maurice Scully: *Steps*, £6.50
1999
  Barbara Guest: *If So, Tell Me* (O/P)
2000
  Tony Lopez: *Data Shadow*, £6.50
  Denise Riley: *Selected Poems*, £9
2001
  Anselm Hollo (ed. & tr.): *Five From Finland*, £7.50
  Lisa Robertson: *The Weather*, £7.50*
2003
  Ken Edwards: *eight + six*, £7.50
  Robert Sheppard: *The Lores*, £7.50
  Lawrence Upton: *Wire Sculptures*, £5
2004
  David Miller: *Spiritual Letters (I-II)*, £6.50
  Redell Olsen: *Secure Portable Space*, £7.50
  Peter Riley: *Excavations*, £9
2005
  Allen Fisher: *Place*, £18
  Tony Baker: *In Transit*, £7.50

2006

Jeff Hilson: *stretchers*, £7.50

Maurice Scully: *Sonata*, £8.50

Maggie O'Sullivan: *Body of Work*, £15

2007

Sarah Riggs: *chain of minuscule decisions in the form of a feeling*, £7.50

Carol Watts: *Wrack*, £7.50

2008

Jeff Hilson (ed.): *The Reality Street Book of Sonnets*, £15

2009

Peter Jaeger: *Rapid Eye Movement*

Allan Kolski Horwitz & Ken Edwards (ed.): *Botsotso*, £12.50

* co-published with New Star Books, Vancouver, BC

4Packs series

1996

1: *Sleight of Foot* (Champion, Kidd, Tarlo, Thurston), £5

1998

2: *Vital Movement* (Brown, Chalmers, Higgins, Lightman), £5

1999

3: *New Tonal Language* (Farrell, Matthews, Perril,Sutherland), £5

2002

4: *Renga+* (Barker, James/Manson, Kennedy), £5

Narrative series

1998

Ken Edwards: *Futures*, £6.99

2005

John Hall: *Apricot Pages*, £6.50

David Miller: *The Dorothy and Benno Stories*, £7.50

Douglas Oliver: *Whisper 'Louise'*, £15

2007

Ken Edwards: *Nostalgia for Unknown Cities*, £8.50

2008

Paul Griffiths: *let me tell you*, £9

Go to www.realitystreet.co.uk, email info@realitystreet.co.uk or write to the address on the reverse of the title page for updates.

BECOME A REALITY STREET SUPPORTER!

For over 10 years more than 100 individuals and organisations have actively supported Reality Street. The Supporter scheme keeps Reality Street's programme of adventurous writing alive. When you sign up as a Supporter, you receive all titles published in that year, and your name is printed in the back of the books, as below (unless you prefer anonymity). For details, go to www.realitystreet.co.uk or email info@realitystreet.co.uk

Reality Street Supporters who have sponsored this book:

David Annwn
Andrew Brewerton
Paul Buck
Clive Bush
John Cayley
Adrian Clarke
Ian Davidson
Mark Dickinson
Michael Finnissy
Allen Fisher/Spanner
Sarah Gall
Harry Gilonis &
Elizabeth James
Chris Goode
Giles Goodland
Paul Griffiths
Charles Hadfield
Catherine Hales
John Hall
Alan Halsey
Robert Hampson
Jeff Hilson
Fanny Howe
Piers Hugill
L Kiew
Steve Lake
Peter Larkin
Richard Leigh
Tony Lopez
Aodhan McCardle
Ian McMillan
Michael Mann
Peter Manson
Deborah Meadows

Mark Mendoza
Peter Middleton
Geraldine Monk
Alice Notley
Marjorie Perloff
Pete & Lyn
Tom Quale
Peter Quartermain
Josh Robinson
Lou Rowan
Will Rowe
Anthony Rudolf
James Russell
Barry Schwabsky
Maurice Scully
Robert Sheppard
Peterjon & Yasmin Skelt
Julius Smit
Hazel Smith
Valerie & Geoffrey Soar
Harriet Tarlo
Andrew Taylor
Tony Trehy
Keith Tuma
Lawrence Upton
Catherine Wagner
Sam Ward
Carol Watts
John Welch/The Many Press
Susan Wheeler
John Wilkinson
Tim Woods
Anonymous x 7